Rules for Living in Tokyo

Published 1874

Edited by Endo Kido

Translated by Eric Shahan

Tokyo Daily Newspaper
Volume 969

Tokyo Daily Newspaper
Volume 969
March 14th (Year unknown circa 1873-1879)

There was a fire in Small Boat Town, Tokyo on March 14th. During the incident fire a woman was found dressed as a man. She was wearing purple cotton trousers, a hood over her head and woven grass sandal along with an embroidered Hanten, short winter coat. She was moving around the scene here and there observing the actions of the officials and the firefighters along with the men.

A Junsa police officer noticed that a man was moving like a woman and called out for her to halt. After learning her name and address it turns out she is an ex-geisha from Osaka Town. She is the adopted daughter of a man named Nakamura Seisuke, who also goes by various other names including Hotei Kan, Tomimoto Anwa Taifu. The woman was escorted to the police box and ordered to pay a fine.

Art by Utagawa Yoshiiku 歌川芳幾 (1833 ~1904)

Translator's Introduction

The Meiji Restoration in 1868 ended the nearly 300-year control of the government by the Tokugawa Shogunate. The new Meiji government completely reshaped Japan and made sweeping changes to how everyday citizens lived their lives.

Reorganization of the Whole Country

An 1872 map showing the 72 prefectures

Up until 1868 Japan was divided into Han, or Domains, each ruled by a Daimyo, feudal lord, that collected taxes and had their own army. In 1871 the government decided to implement *Haihan-chiken* 廃藩置県, or the scrapping of the feudal domain system in favor of a reduced number of prefectures. The Daimyo, who headed each domain, had to return their authority to the Meiji Emperor. In exchange, they were left in control of their former domains, albeit as non-hereditary governors.

Initially, the feudal domains were converted to 305 prefectures. They were gradually reduced as follows:

1871 – 75 Prefectures
1872 – 72 Prefectures
1873 – 63 Prefectures
1875 – 62 Prefectures
1876 – 38 Prefectures

However, after the 1876 decision there was a lot of grumbling about how some prefectures were extremely large, with corresponding questions about how to manage such a large area. Therefore in 1889 the number was increased to 45 prefectures, with Okinawa being added in 1879 and Hokkaido in 1886.

Social Classes

The social hierarchy changed as well during the Meiji period. During the Edo Era (1600-1867,) there was a feudal class system embodied in the Shi-No-Ko-Sho 士農工商, or four divisions of society, under which society was divided as follows:

Shi– The Samurai (around 10% of the population) were the rulers, superior in both their status and the example they set.
No – The farmers (around 80% of the population) were second because they produced the food necessary for society.
Ko – The craftsmen and artisans (around 5%) were placed next since they made things for people to use.
Sho – Merchants (around 5%) were ranked the lowest since they sold things made by others.

In addition, about 1% of the population was in the priesthood and another 1% were considered outcasts. However, with the Meiji Restoration in 1868, Japanese could change their social class, where they lived and their occupation.

Katana

Beginning in 1869 laws were being debated regarding eliminating the wearing of Katana. Should the new government abolish the wearing of the long and short Katana, the symbol of Samurai rank? The law was controversial with proponents arguing along the lines of "Move away from barbaric practices," while those in favor of maintaining the tradition argued, "Abandoning wearing the Katana will erode fighting spirt and degrade the vitality of our Imperial Country."

Eventually, the *Sword Abolishment Edict* 廃刀令 was issued by the Meiji government in March of 1876. It prohibited carrying swords in public, with the exception of former Daimyo, the military and police. Violators would have their Katana confiscated. The illustration above, from the April 4th, 1876 edition of the *Tokyo Illustrated Newspaper* shows a constable confronting a travelling ex-Samurai, who is still wearing a long and short sword. The final reasoning given was, "Since a police force had been established, wearing a sword for self-defense is no longer necessary."

Removing the Samurai's Topknot

The Meiji Empoeror in 1873

Zangiri hairstyle

Since ancient times men and women in Japan have had long hair, either tied up in some fashion or allowed to hang down. Traditionally, to cut your hair short was an indication of a separation from society, repentance, or punishment. Danpatsu, or shaving the head, was something done before setting out as a travelling monk or indicative of official punishment. Even today when Sumo wrestlers retire, they hold a ceremony to remove the Chonmage topknot, signifying their retirement.

In Meiji 4 (1871) a *Sanpatsu Datto Rei* was issued by the government. This meant that for official meetings between the Japanese governments and representatives of other nations they would have their hair "free," as in not tied in a Chonmage, in addition to not wearing a sword. Further, dignitaries from other nations would be received in a room prepared with, "chairs with high legs" and a "table." Everyone would also receive guests while wearing shoes.

This rule only applied to government officials, and the general populous was both quite attached to the Chonmage style and resistant to the Sanpatsu, "free hair" style. However, in 1873 the Meiji Emperor had his picture taken with his hair in a Western style. This led to a boom in Zangiri and other Western style haircuts.

The reasoning behind these changes was the Meiji governments desire to rapidly become "modern" and civilized." Foreigners had often commented that the Chonmage hairstyle was representative of Japan's undeveloped culture, thus the Meiji government sought to abandon this old practice.

Police and Criminal Law

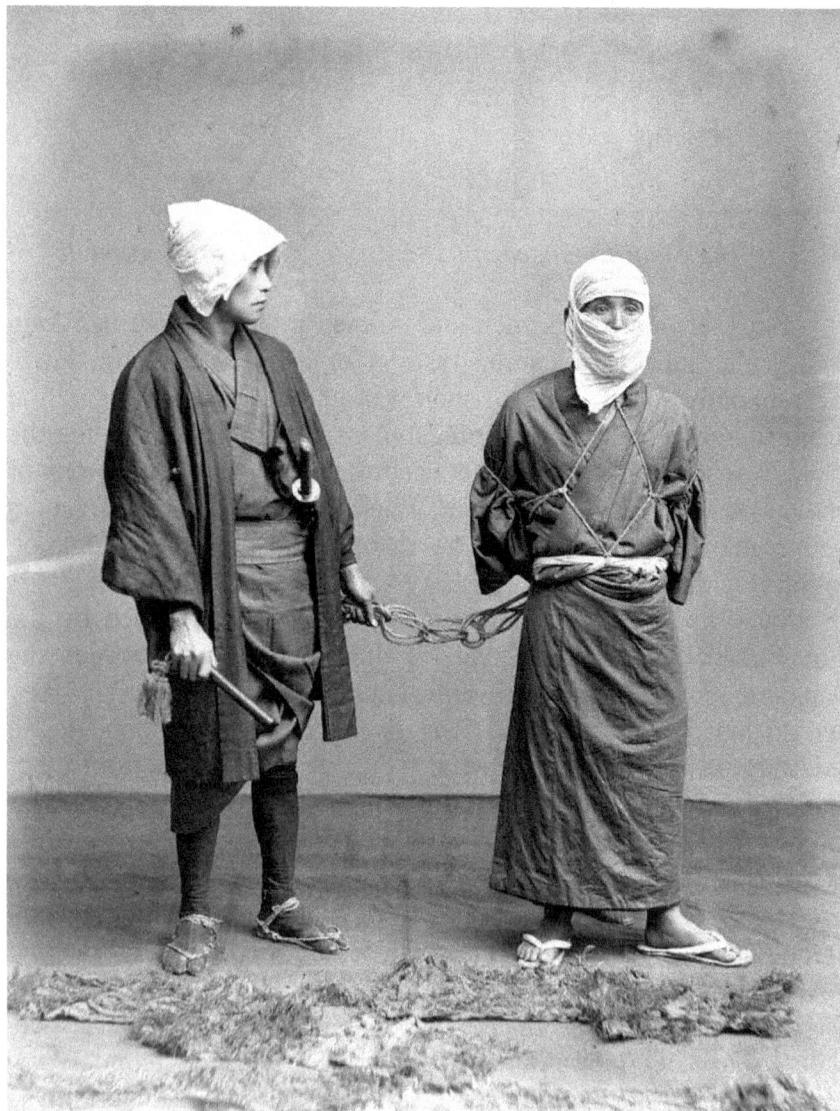

Photograph from the late 19th re-creating how criminals were transported after being arrested.

Earliest Police in Japan

The earliest example of policing can be found in the Kojiki, written in the 8th century.

In the age of the gods, Ninigi-no-Mikoto 瓊瓊杵尊 *,the grandson of the sun goddess Amaterasu and the great-grandfather of Japan's first emperor, descended from Heaven. He brought rice and order to earth. On his journey to earth he was protected by many deities, including Aatsukume no Mikoto, who was armed with the Stone Quiver on his back, Kobu Sword on his belt, Heavenly Wave bow in his hand, which was nocked with the True Deer Child arrow.*

-History Of Aichi Prefecture Police

Edo Era Police

In the Edo Era (1600-1868) the police stations were called Machi Bugyosho and the administer of such a station was the Machi Bugyo, a high-ranking Samurai. This Samurai acted as the Chief of Police as well as the chief prosecutor and judge. There were around 16 of these officials spread out over Japan and Edo city had two, North Station and South Station.

Next in rank under the Machi Bugyo were the Yoriki, who were lower ranked Samurai constables. Each police station in Edo had 25 Yoriki. Under the Yoriki were Doshin, Patrol Officers. The Doshin were also Samurai, however they were of a lower rank. They patrolled the streets, conducted investigations, and also served as prison guards, which meant they assisted with executions. They had the most direct contact with the Chonin, "city folk." There were a hundred Doshin assigned to each police station in Edo. The population of Edo around that time was around 500,000 city folk, with the total for all the area covered by Edo city being a million people.

With so few official police patrolling the streets, the Doshin employed Okappiki 岡っ引, Informant-assistants. The Okappiki were typically former criminals, who were given leniency in exchange for working as assistants and informants. The Okappiki were non-Samurai so they were not permitted to carry lethal weapons, though most carried a "pocketknife" as well as rope and a Jutte truncheon. Their official name was Goyokiki 御用聞き "Official Listeners" however they were called different things in different regions. The Okappiki name was actually quite derogatory as they were former criminals and sometimes resorted to bullying citizens for "protection money." There were around 500 of them in employ.

Meiji Era Police

Under the Tokugawa Government the main purpose of the police department can, in no uncertain terms, be said to have been less about,

Protecting the citizenry and ensuring their enrichment and happiness and more about maintaining the stability of the Tokugawa Bakufu Government.
-Ninety Years of Police Department Martial Arts History
警視庁武道九十年史 1962.

In the early days just after the Meiji Restoration, a system for policing was no longer in place. Soldiers from the various victorious forces that had participated in the Boshin conflict began acting, "Bojaku-bujin 傍若無人, or behaving outrageously." In response to this there were various types of measures enacted that, through a trial-and-error method, ended up with the current Japanese Police system. The following five stages roughly outline how this occurred.

Shichu Torishimari Jidai 市中取締時代
Citywide Control Era

The first method of modern policing the Meiji government tried was called the Citywide Control Era. On February 17th of the 4th year of Keio, 1868 the former Machibugyo, Mr. Ishikawa Toshimura (?-1868) was ordered to take charge of keeping order in the city until the new police system began. Unfortunately, he committed Seppuku on his first day of work and the job fell to a subordinate.

Hanhei Jidai 藩兵時代
The Era of Using Ex-Domain Soldiers

In April of 1868 the government enlisted troops from a total of twelve areas including Kii, Choshu, Satsuma, Bizen and Saga and called the collection Hanhei, or Domain Troops. The Hahei were patrolled in groups to maintain order and protect the citizenry.

Unfortunately, despite having been assigned the important task of maintaining public safety the Hanhei began to dine and drink without paying, threaten people with impunity and, in the worst cases, robbed and stole. Therefore, the Hanhei were disbanded.

In November of 1868, still the first year of Meiji, 200 soldiers from Oshi Han were provisionally dispatched to Tokyo as peacekeepers and the method for maintaining the peace began to be reformed.

Fuhei Jidai 府兵時代
The Era of Tokyo Metropolitan Soldiers

In December of 1868 soldiers from thirty domains were selected and brought to Tokyo. They were then reorganized into the Fuhei, or metropolitan soldiers, and assigned to a part of the city. This system spread to other areas of Japan as well and lasted until 1871 whereupon the Ministry of Justice (1871-1948) was founded, and the police were split from the military.

Rasotsu Jidai 邏卒時代
The Patrolling Soldier Era

By 1870, many regions of Japan found that the Fuhei system was lacking and were seeking a more comprehensive solution to policing. The Rasotsu System was established in October of 1871, which was standard uniformed soldiers, who were all trained the same way. While they initially patrolled with swords this was soon abandoned in favor of a standard 90 cm Konbo 棍棒 or club.

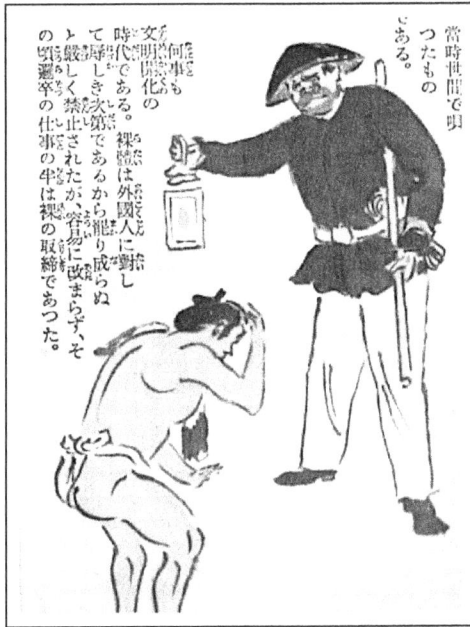

A Rasotsu Patrol Officer wearing the traditional white slacks and carrying a Konbo. He is confronting a man in violation of the 1871 ordinance against being inappropriately dressed.

The ban on wearing a sword for Rasotsu had the unexpected consequence of causing the number of applicants to fall by half. Apparently, the appeal of becoming a Rasotsu was the fact that one could wear a sword. The general consensus was that was that they went from being a Samurai (armed with a sword) to something akin to a prison guard (armed only with a club).

Junsa Jidai 巡査時代
Era of the Patrol Officer

In the 1870's Kawaji Toshiyoshi 川路利良 （1834~1879） travelled to France and returned with an idea of how to model Japan's police department after European and American systems. He later served as the first head of the national police force.

川路 利良 Kawaji Toshiyoshi （1834-1879）

In 1872 the position of Junsa 巡査, or Patrol Officer, was established replacing the Rasotsu. The following are some facts regarding this early type of Japanese police officer.

The Requirements to Become a Junsa Patrol Officer:

- Between the ages of 20-40
- Healthy and over 5 Shaku (165cm) in height
- To agree with the laws of Japan and the Police and have a working knowledge of Japanese History
- To be able to read typical documents and be capable of writing
- A person in control of themselves and able to show restraint

Salary for Junsa Police Officers

- Pay starting at 10 Yen for a First Class Junsa and down to 4 Yen for a Fourth Class Junsa per month.
- Depending on ability and response to crimes pay can increase
- If a fine is set, half the money will be paid to the officer.
- Further, if an arsonist is stopped an additional 20 Sen will be paid
- If the officer recovers a drowned body an additional 50 Sen will be paid.
- If a robber is caught, then 10 Yen will be paid.
- Summer and winter uniform provided and shoe allowance of 3 Yen 50 Sen.

To put the salary in contemporary terms, "1 Yen" was equivalent to about $200. Around this time a schoolteacher made 8 ~ 9 Yen per month with an experienced worker or carpenter around 20 Yen. Thus, a Junsa Patrol Officer's salary was fairly low and there was a saying that went, "No one is going to marry a Junsa!" The Junsa, who wore western style clothing, began to be referred to as Omawari San, or *Those That Walk About* by the populace.

Though initially unarmed, in the 7th year of Meiji (1874,) Junsa were again authorized to wear a sword due to anti-government activity. Some of the police were even formed into fighting units and engaged in battle in the Satsuma Rebellion of 1877. Eventually a Taiken Keikan, or Police Officers Armed With Swords, division was created, though members were almost exclusively from former Samurai families, excluding police officers from the general populace.

Junsa Patrol Officers assisted by a rickshaw driver apprehend a highwayman. Osaka Illustrated Newspaper. (19th century.)

Reasoning Behind the New Laws

In 1870, the new Meiji government issued a set of laws for minor infractions. These were based on a combination of Japanese law, such as the ones found in *The100 Judicial Decrees* 御定書百箇条 written in 1745, as well as Western and Chinese laws. The Western laws were incorporated into the new Japanese legal system because of the Meiji governments tendency to craft policy with a pro-Western influence. This was termed *Move away from Asia, Accept European Influence* 脱亜入欧.

The goal of the new civil code was to modernize and Westernize Japan's culture. Other terms used to justify the new policies are:

文明開化 *Bunmei Kaikaka*
Civilization and enlightenment. This was a key phrase in Japan's Westernization movement. The phrase could also be translated as "opening up to civilization."

見苦敷風習 *Migurushiki-Fushu*
Describing Early Meiji Era traditions as unsightly and shameful.

卑敷風俗 *Hishiki Fushu/Narifuri*
Like the previous term, this phrase also laments Japan's indecent cultural traditions.

御国体 *Gokokutai*
This phrase refers to the Nation of Japan as a Whole, its image. This term was used to indicate the *Migurushi-Fushu* were adversely affecting the image of Japan on the world stage.

裸体 *Ratai*
Naked bodies. The Japanese tradition of carpenters, rickshaw drivers, porters and steeplejacks of working in just a Fundoshi loincloth, was referred to as "naked." There was an additional source of "nakedness" with the public bath houses. Most Japanese did not have a bath at their house and used public baths. It was quite

Implementation of the New Laws For Minor Infractions

The central government first crafted 90 regulations in 1872 and in the following year, they were distributed to all the prefectures. These regulations were considered a guideline to be adapted by the local government according to their circumstances. These regulations were enforced by the newly created police force, known as Junsa Patrol Officers. These patrol officers would spot violations and issue punishment or fines on the spot. The regulations were based on how the French police handled minor breaks in the law. It was also influenced by London, Shanghai and Hong Kong police procedures.

A French legal expert named Gustave Émile Boissonade de Fontarabie (1825 –1910) was invited to Japan to assist with crafting Japan's civil code. Boissonade lived in Japan from 1873 to 1895 teaching at the Law School of the Ministry of Justice. He worked with Ume Kenjiro and Hozumi Nobushige on drafting Japan's new criminal and civil code.

These regulations were intended as a stopgap measure and used from 1872 until 1885 where they were replaced by more refined system called Police Violation Crime 違警罪. These laws were divided into 3 categories of infraction, light and severe. The Police Violation Crimes system was kept until 1948 where it was replaced by the Minor Crime Law.

Each area hired printers to make illustrated versions in order for the regulations to be made easily available to the public.

Rules For Living In Tokyo

This book contains the "sample" 90 regulations and is titled, *Disregarding the Rules・Mistakenly Violating the Rules The Complete Illustrated Guide* and was published on July 7th of Meiji 7 (1874.) For clarity I have titled it *Rules for Living in Tokyo*. Later, other prefecture adjusted the laws (adding or subtracting) to suit the needs of their area and hired printers to make illustrated versions in order for the regulations to be made easily available to the public. In addition, the local governments paid for several hundred copies to be distributed at no cost to locals.

These regulations were intended as a stopgap measure and were the law from 1872 until 1885 when they were replaced by more refined system called *Police Violation Crime* 違警罪. The *Police Violation Crimes* system was kept until 1948 when it was replaced by the *Minor Crime Law*.

Disregarding the Rules
Mistakenly Violating the Rules

明治七年七月　　奎文房發兌　　遠藤　喜道　編輯

違式　詿違　御條目圖解　全

The Complete Illustrated Guide
July 7th Meiji 7 (1874)
Edited by Endo Kido

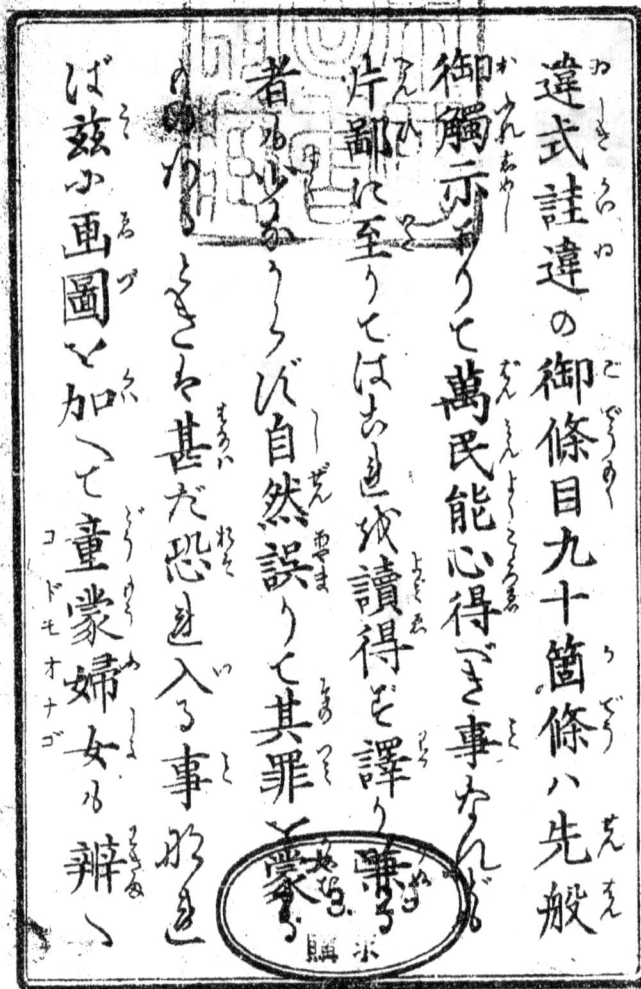

違式詿違の御條目九十箇條ハ先般御觸示ありて萬民能心得べき事なれど片郡に至りてはより迴城讀得ぞ譯り者かなかるうらび自然誤りて其罪さや甚だ恐れ迴入る事があば茲小画圖と加へて童蒙婦女ね辨へ

There are a total of 90 Regulations in *Ishiki・Kaii*, or *Disregarding the Rules・Mistakenly Violating the Rules*. Since they have been recently introduced it is the responsibility of all the citizens to learn them. Those that do not are in danger of being perceived as unenlightened and crass.

It is natural that people will make mistakes but this will be detrimental to your household. To make them clear I have included illustrations so that even a young girl can understand them.

2

明治七年甲戌六月　　遠藤喜道謹誌

易うしやんき次依て衆庶必らし
き道と求めく以て常に坐右に置能
々記臆して忘却をる事かうれ

Members of the populous should acquire a copy of these regulations, keep it close at hand and memorize them. By doing so there will be no danger of forgetting.
Written in June of Meiji 7 (1874)

By the Editor
Endo Kido

第二百五十六號

各地方違式詿違條例別冊之通被定候條此旨布告候事

Directive 256

Each area should make copies of *Disregarding the Rules・Mistakenly Violating the Rules* available and distribute them to the public.

但地方之便宜ニ依リ斟酌増減
之廉ハ警保寮ヘ可伺出且條
例掲示之儀モ同寮之指揮ヲ
可受事

明治六年七月十九日　太政大臣三條實美

However, each area may, according to its convenience, increase or decrease the number of regulations as that area sees fit. This will be decided by the local police department who has a duty to post such regulations appropriately.

July of Meiji 6 (1873) Central Government

内務省　達書　第二十五號

違式詿違條例之儀ハ既ニ明治六年第

二百五十六號ヲ以御布告相成候處元來

風俗習慣ヲ變更スルハ甚至難之事件殊

三縣内ト雖モ各地之人情彼是異同モ有之

一朝一夕ニ可被行儀ニ無之然ルニ概ニ之

ヲ施行シ自然人民之苦情怨嗟ヲ釀シ

Ministry of Home Affairs
Directive #25

The regulations titled *Disregarding the Rules* and *Mistakenly Violating the Rules* were distributed in Meiji 6 (1873) in Directive #256. Clearly, changing the manners and customs of a society is an extremely difficult business even within one prefecture. Each locality within that prefecture will say "we do things this way" while another area will say "we do things that way." Some things are the same and others are different.

It is not something that can be implemented over the course of one morning and one evening. It goes without saying that when implemented it will naturally draw complaints, anger and bitterness from our citizens. Though this occurred it is contrary to the original intent of establishing these regulations.

候様之儀有之候テハ抑條例設立之本旨ニ
悖リ候ニ付三府五港ヲ除クノ外各地方ニ於
テ成丈懇切説諭シ漸次施行之積リヲ以テ
宜敷時勢人情之適度斟酌之上取捨増減
安寧保護之實相貫キ候樣厚ク可致注意
此旨爲心得相達候事

明治七年三月九日

These changes are being implemented not just in the Sanpu-Goko, or the Three Metropolitan Areas (Tokyo Kyoto and Osaka) and the Five Ports Open to Foreign Ships (Yokohama, Kobe, Nagasaki, Niigata and Hakodate) but also in each region of Japan. While keeping in mind the spirit of this new age, these regulations are being carefully explained and gradually implemented. An appropriate level of leeway is included so that regulations may be added or removed as necessary to preserve stability and to take into account the realities of the situation in each area.

With careful consideration the underlying purpose of these regulations can be achieved.

March 20th of Meiji 7 (1874)

違式詿違條例

第一條　違式の罪を犯す者ハ七十五錢より少かるべからず百五十錢より多かるべからず　贖金と追徵を

第二條　詿違の罪を犯す者ハ六錢二厘五毛より少かるべからず十二錢五厘より多かるべからず　贖金及追徵を

Disregarding the Rules・Mistakenly Violating the Rules

#1

Any person violating *Disregarding the Rules* will pay a fine of at least 75 Sen to not more than 150 Sen.[1]

#2

Any person violating *Mistakenly Violating the Rules* will pay a fine of at least 6 Sen 2.5 Rin to not more than 12 Sen 5 Rin.

---

[1] *Rules for Living in Tokyo* did not have an illustration for #1&2 these are from *Rules for Living in Osaka.*

Translator's Note:	
These are some of the coins used in the Meiji Era.	
	円 Yen
	銭 Sen 1/100th of a Yen
	厘 Rin 1/10th of a Sen

In the 10th year of Meiji a carpenter made about 40 Sen a day and in 1987 a carpenter made about 14,000 ¥ or 140$ a day so 1 Sen was about 350¥ or 3.50$. These days a Japanese carpenter can make 15,000 to 25,000 (150 ~ 250$) a day depending on experience.

第三條

違式詿違の罪と犯し事左の如し

無力の者ハ實決をら
アタヘキンヲイダスコトヌデキヌマツシキモノ

一 違式 笞罪 一十より少からうひ 二十より多からうず

一 詿違 拘留 一日より少からうひ 二日より多からうず

但 二罪とる 適宜懲役か換ふ

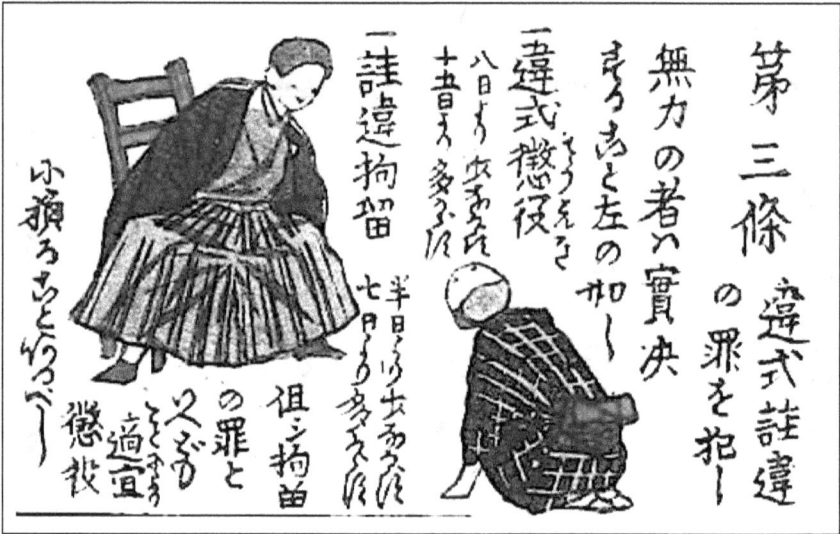

3

Any person who has committed a *Disregarding the Rules* or *Mistakenly Violating the Rules* crime and is "without power" (does not have the means to pay the fine) will be handled as follows:

- Violations of *Disregarding the Rules* will be whipped from a minimum of 10 times to not more than 20 times

- Violations of Mistakenly Violating the Rules will be put in jail for a minimum of one day to a maximum of two days. However if it is the second offense then the penalty is switched to imprisonment with hard labor.[2]

---

[2] *Rules for Living in Tokyo* did not have an illustration for #1&2 these are from *Rules for Living in Osaka*.

Translator's Note:

Punishment by whipping was done with a kind of half-whip half-stick called "the end of a broom" 箒尻. It was about 60 cm long and about 9 cm in diameter. The core was a piece of bamboo split into several sections, then wrapped with hemp paper and then bound with Kanzeyori 観世捻, a kind of paper string. Sometimes leather was wrapped around the handle.

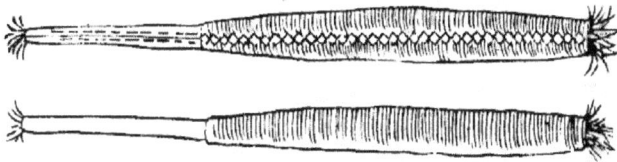

Illustration of the "whip" called a Chida or Muchiuchi

Illustration of a whipping being carried out from *Rules for Living in Osaka*. Strikes were done on the back arms legs and buttocks.

Picture of an Edo Era *Roya* 牢屋, or prison
Sendai Domain 仙台藩

Late 19th century illustration showing the inside of a Japanese prison. The prisoners had a strict hierarchy. The top prisoner sits on a stack of half a dozen Tatami mats while the lower ranked prisoners sit on the bare ground. New prisoners are presented and stripped of any valuables.

第四條　違式并ニ詿違の罪により取上

ごき物品ハ贖金と科をその外別に没

収の申渡しと形にぐ

第五條　違式詿違の罪を犯し一人に損

失と蒙らしむる時ハ先其損失に當

る償金と出さしめ後か贖金と命じ

ぐ

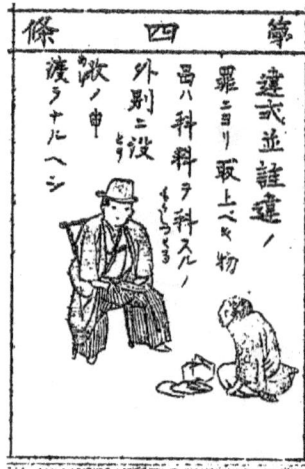

#4

Any items taken in the course of either Disregarding the Rules or Mistakenly Violating the Rules will be confiscated and be used to determine the money for atonement (the fine.)[3]

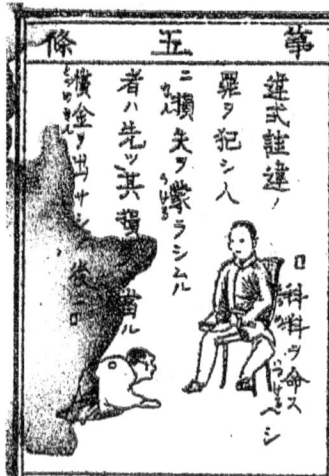

#5

Anyone found guilty of either Disregarding the Rules or Mistakenly Violating the Rules that involved damage or loss to property, will first have to pay for the damage or loss of property. After that you will have to pay money for atonement (a fine.)

---

[3] *Rules for Living in Tokyo* did not have an illustration for 4 & 5 so these two illustrations are from *Rules for Living in Kyoto.*

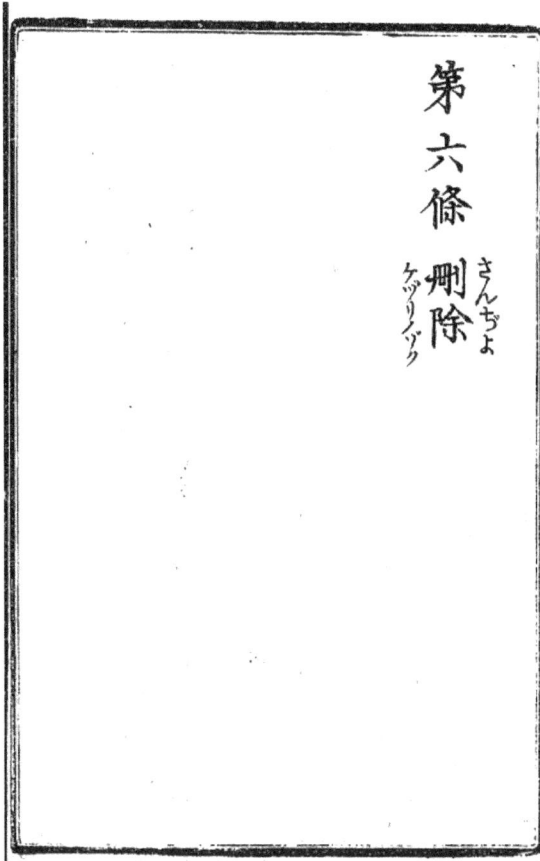

第六條 削除

#6

This regulation has been erased.[4]

---

[4] This regulation was originally regarding land rights but was dropped in Meiji 7. In Meiji 9 the following article replaced it.

#6

If a person is guilty of Disregarding the Rules but the infraction is mild, then the fines for Mistakenly Violating the Rules can be applied.

Sign:

魚

"Fish"

第七條

贋造の飲食物并に腐敗の食物と知て賤賣そる者

The Following Offences are Classified as:
Disregarding the Rules

#7

Any person selling fake food or drink as well as anyone knowingly selling rotten food is in violation.

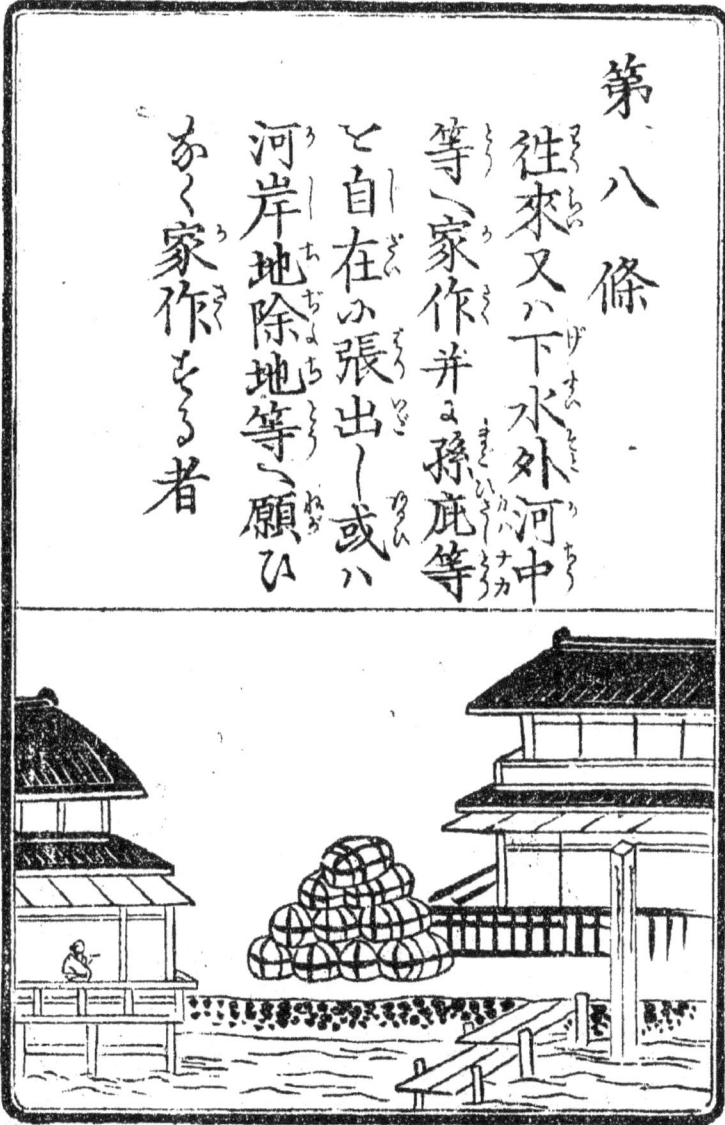

第八條
往來又ハ下水外河中
等ヘ家作并ニ孫庇等
と自在の張出し或ハ
河岸地除地等ニ願ひ
なく家作をる者

#8

Building a house in a place where people pass through or building a house that extends over a public waterway is a violation. This includes building an extension over a body of water, a balcony, an extra room over the water, or any other construction that implies you are the owner of a particular section. This also applies to people who build alongside the river or on public land without permission.

第九條

春画及び其類の諸器物と販賣する者

#9
Any person selling Shunga, or books with erotic images or any related paraphernalia is in violation.

Translator's Note:

Shunga are erotic pictures and stories that were also referred to as laughing pictures. The "related paraphernalia" included medicines like Chomeigan 長命丸 "Long Life Pills" a kind of Edo Era Viagra.

 | 長命丸 Chomeigan "Long Life Pills"

Chomeigan was derived from a medicine imported from Holland and was sold at a shop called Yotsume, The Fourth Shop. According to the book *Relationships Between Men and Women in the Edo Era* the researcher and author Dr. Tanaka Kogai 田中香涯, 1874-1944 says,

There were a great many aphrodisiacs with names like Jeweled Relaxation Pills, As You Desire Pills, Man and Horse Pills, Yin Yang Pills and so on. They were derived from Chinese herbal medicines. Chomeigan was a mix of cloves, "dragon brains" (borneol) 竜脳 pepper and other ingredients.

Left and following page: An Edo Era illustration showing a woman selling a package of male vitality medicine.
Right: Advertisement for Yonbanme The Fourth Shop.

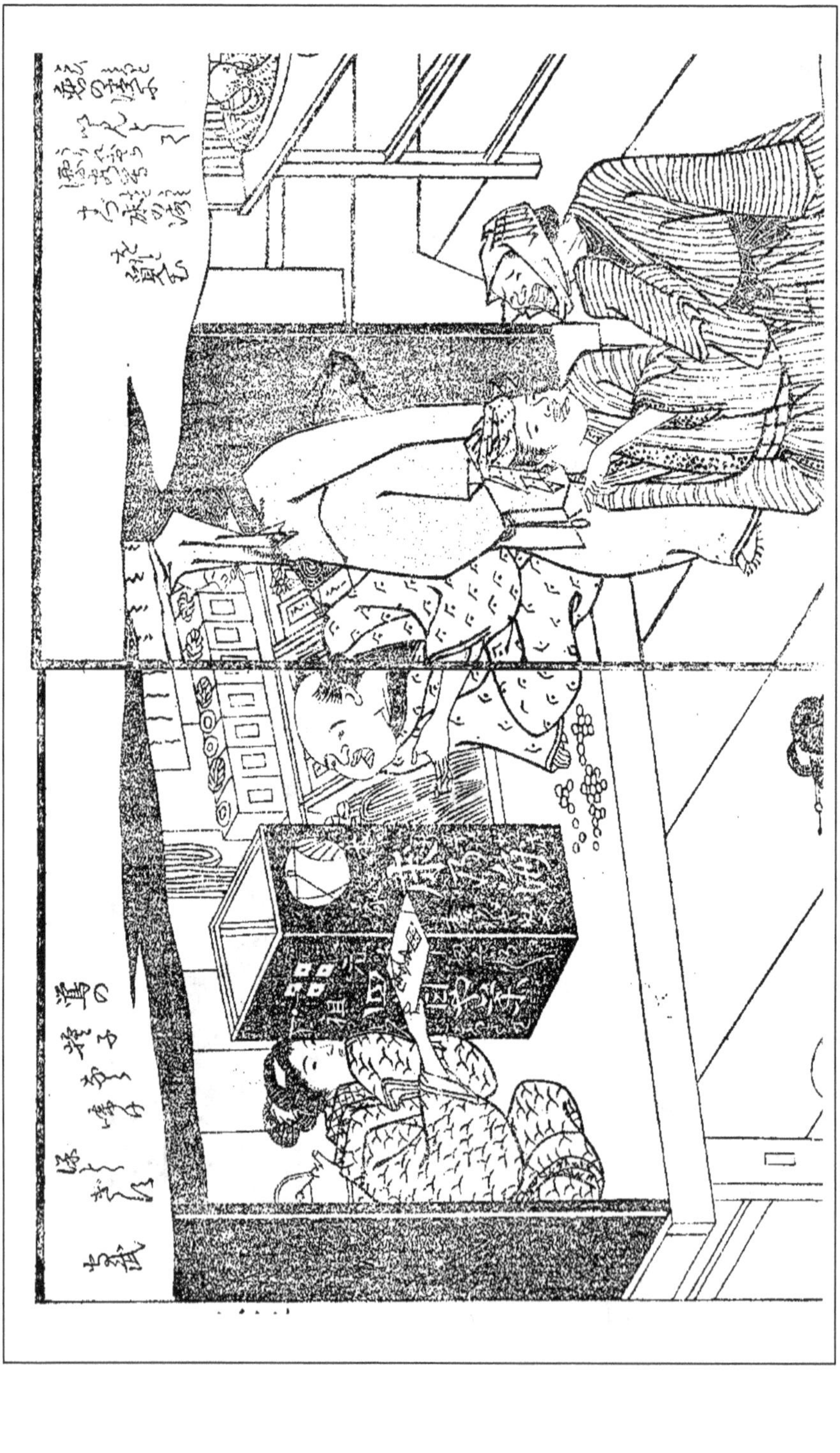

第十條

病牛死牛其他病死の禽獣と知りて販賣をする者

Sign:

牛肉

"beef"

#10
Any person selling the meat of a cow or horse that died of disease is in violation. This also applies those who knowingly sell the meat of birds or other wild animals that died of disease.

身體ヘ刺繍をなし者

第十一條

#11

Any person who engraves or embroiders a person's body is in violation.

Translator's Note: Horimono "Engraving" and Shishu "Embroidery" were two ways of referring to tattooing. Irezumi, or tattooing, existed in Japan at least since the 3rd century AD and it was described in Chinese texts at the time. Beginning in the peaceful Edo Era, tattooing began to re-emerge. It began in the brothels in Kyoto in the early 1600's.

The courtesans began engraving the names of their clients into their arms with razor blades or needles and then rubbing ink into the cuts. It then spread to couples seeking to show their bond through Iribokuro, tattooed "moles" on the hands. By the late 1600's men began tattooing dramatic phrases and simple designs on their arms and chests to intimidate people. By the late 1700's more elaborate tattoos of human figures, dragons, masks, severed heads and various monsters and deities could be seen. By the 1800's most palanquin bearers, steeplejacks, fire fighters, porters and other such people who worked "naked," as in wearing only a loin cloth, had extensive tattooing.

The Edo Era Bakufu government passed two laws banning Irezumi, one in 1810 and again in 1842. The reasoning was, "scarring one's body on purpose is shameful." In 1872 the Meiji Government banned tattooing. The reasoning was, "Scaring the body given to you by your mother and father with images of flowers, birds and pictures of people is shameful. It is embarrassing for foreigners to see this. Also, some prisoners who received tattoos as punishment cover them up with art, thereby concealing their crimes."

With the new law enacted, the police issued permits to those who already had tattoos. According to the July 24, 1876 edition of the *Yomiuri Newspaper* the police issued 1700 tattoo permits over the course of two months. It is said there were many women among them.

Self-applied Iribokuro "Matching Moles" Early 1600's	Simple designs done by a semi-professional early 1700's	Elaborate designs by a professional artist. Late 1790 ~1868

第十二條
男女入込の湯戯
渡世をする者

男女
渡湯

第五條
湯屋渡世の
その男女を
混浴せしむる者

#12

Any person operating an Onsen that allows for men and women to bathe together is in violation.

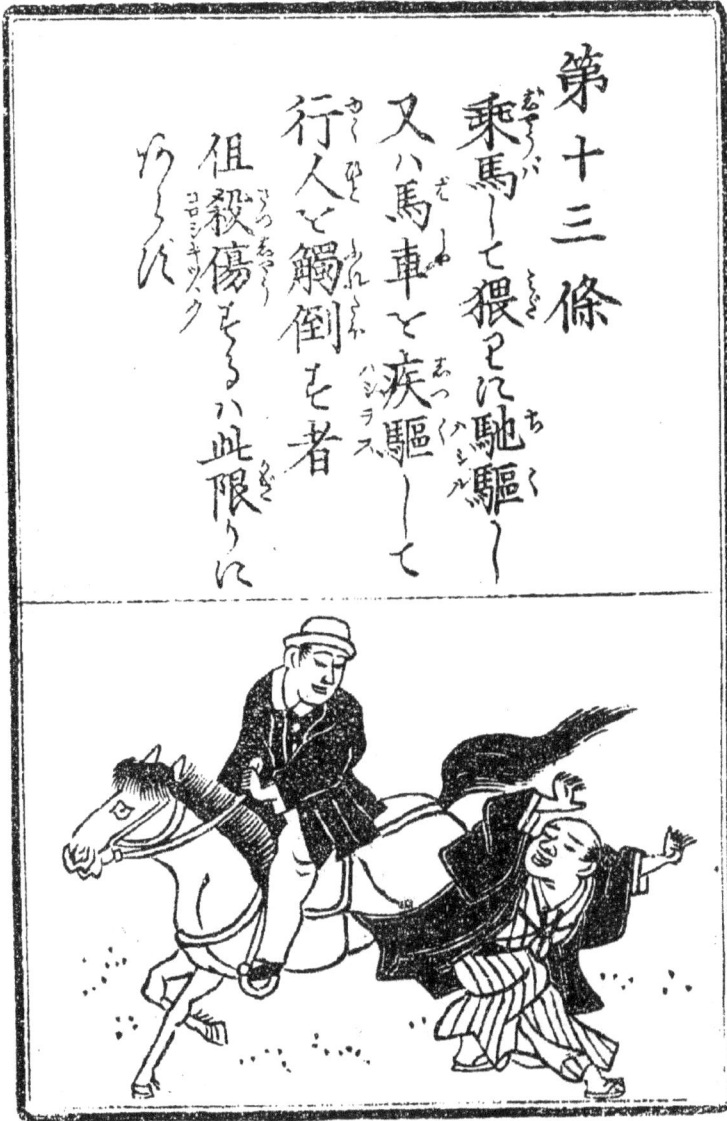

第十三條
乗馬して猥りに馳驅し
又は馬車と疾驅して
行人を觸倒を者
但殺傷をるは此限りに
あらず

#13

Any person riding a horse at a gallop with no good reason, or driving a horse drawn carriage at a high speed who knocks a pedestrian down is in violation.

That being said, this regulation only applies when such an encounter results in serious injury or death.

#14

Any person renting a room to a foreigner without filing a report is in violation.

#15

Any person who is living with a foreigner for personal reasons is in violation.

#16
Any person who drives a horse-drawn carriage at night without a
lantern is in violation.

#17
Any person who carelessly uses fireworks in a crowded residential area is in violation.

#18
Riding a horse to the scene of a fire is a violation unless you are an official.

第十九條
戯＾小往來の常燈
臺と破毀する者

#19
Any person who vandalizes a permanent streetlight placed along a road is in violation.

Translator's Note:

唐
子

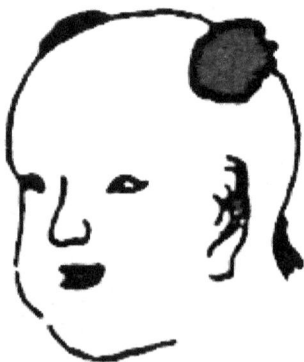

The illustrations in this book depict people with various sections of the hair shaved off. The hair cutting style that leaves clumps of hair on the front, sides and top of the head is known as Karashi, or red pepper. The style was mainly for young boys, so this type of violation may have been common with young boys.

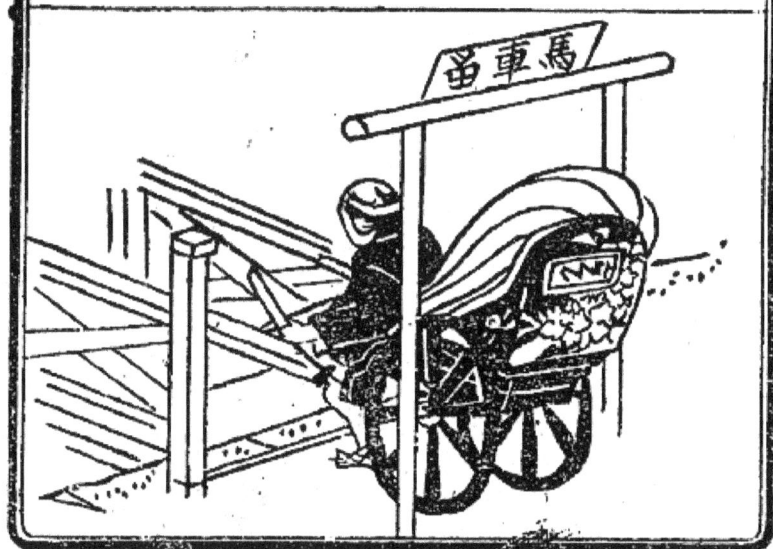

第二十條

馬及び車駕の留の掲示ある道路橋梁を犯して通行をなす者

#20

Any person who ignores a *No Horses, Palanquins or Carts* sign posted at a road or bridge and crosses is in violation.

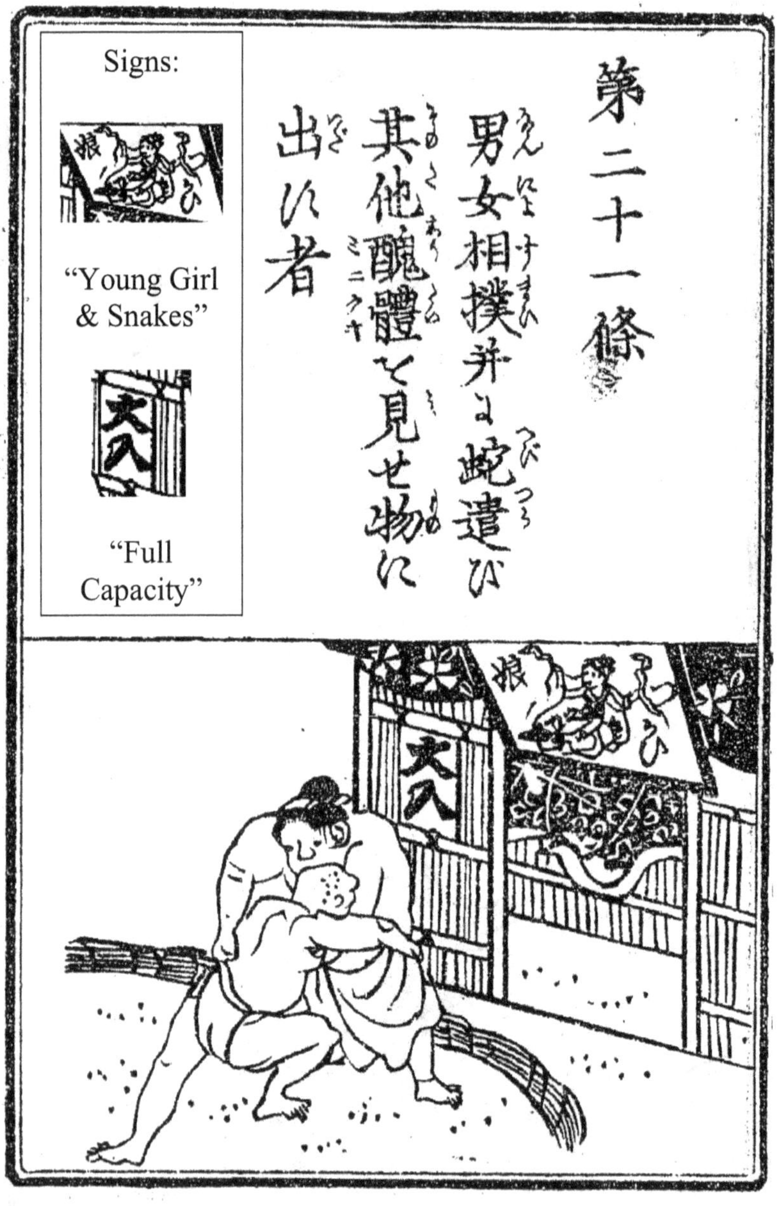

Signs:

"Young Girl & Snakes"

"Full Capacity"

第二十一條

男女相撲并ニ蛇遣び
其他醜體て見せ物に
出し者

#21

Anyone who puts on a Sumo bout between men and women is in violation. This also includes putting on performances by snake handers and any other grotesque displays.

38

Translator's Note:

The first mention of Snake handlers can be found in the 1632 book *Sheets of Grass Paper* 尤の草紙 That describes a carnival-like atmosphere of these performances,

Crazed people, the smell of things rotten, the remnants of a fish market, people of twisted character and snake handlers.

A book of poetry called *The Stones of Mt. Fuji* 富士石, published in Edo in 1677 contained the line, *With the season of frost my snake handling livelihood has become desolate.* The *season of frost* is probably referring to how snakes hibernate in winter and thus making money off performances is impossible. A later book called *Heavenly Peaceful Collection of Laugher* 天和笑委集 describes how snake hander performances were used as a way to draw in spectators to sell medicines. As for the actual performance, *Research in to Sideshows* 見世物研究 says,

Typically snake handers are girls. They first put about ten snakes of all sizes in a woven grass basket and then pull them out one after the other. The real show is when the girls shows the snakes wrapped around her neck and hands.

Illustration from an Edo Manga written by Santo Kyoden in 1801 called *Story of the Curious Crawling Exhibition* 這奇的見世物語

#22

Any person who throws chunks of soil, broken roof tiles, or gravel into a canal or drainage ditch for the purpose of blocking it is in violation.

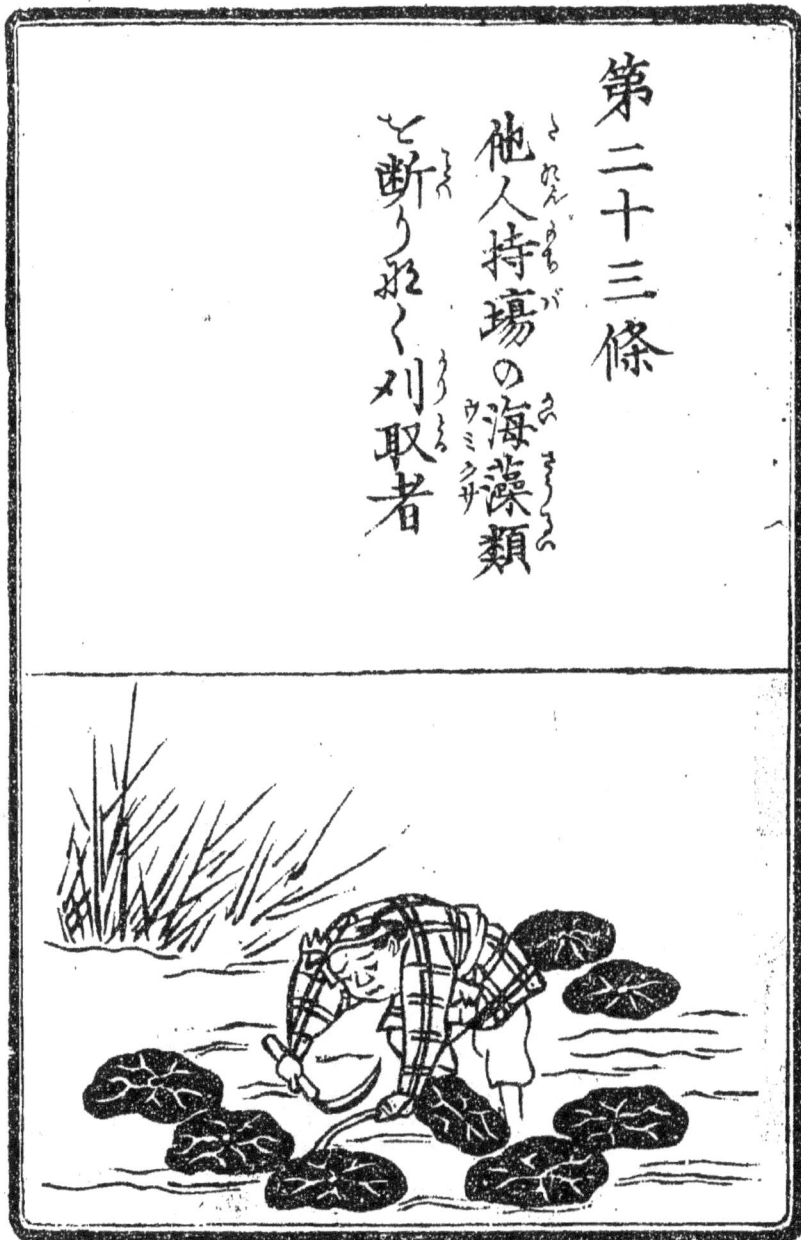

#23

Any person who harvests water plants or seaweed from another person's property without permission is in violation.

第二十四條

他人の持場又ハ免許なき場所か魚藻を設る者

#24
Any person who sets up a fishing net or trap without a permit or on another person's property is in violation.

第二十五條

一 毒薬井ニ激烈氣物ヲ用ヒ魚鳥ヲ捕ル者

#25

Using poisons or other "violently reacting materials" to catch birds or fish is a violation.[5]

---

[5] "Violently reacting materials" refers to explosives.

第二十六條

他人分の田水ハ勿論組

合持の田水と断て勿く

自恣に我田か引入る

者

#26

It goes without saying it is a violation to divert the flow of water from another person's field to your own. In addition, any person who redirects the water meant for a community managed field to their own personal field is in violation.

#27

Any person entering another person's property and harvesting bamboo shoots or mushrooms without permission is in violation.

#28

Any person who rips the notices off public information boards or vandalizes the board itself is in violation.

第二十九條

堤を壊ち又ハ断りぬく
他人の田圃と堀者

#29

Any person who destroys a river embankment or digs a trench in order to bring water from another person's field without permission is in violation.

第三十條

道式内ハ菜蔬豆類と
植或ハ汚物を積往來
と妨ぐる者

#30

Planting vegetables or bean in an area that is considered part of the road is a violation. This regulation also includes stacking trash by the road. If you block the road doing either of the above you are in violation.

#31

Harvesting ripe rice or seedlings from another village's or another person's field is a violation. This includes any crops harvested without permission.

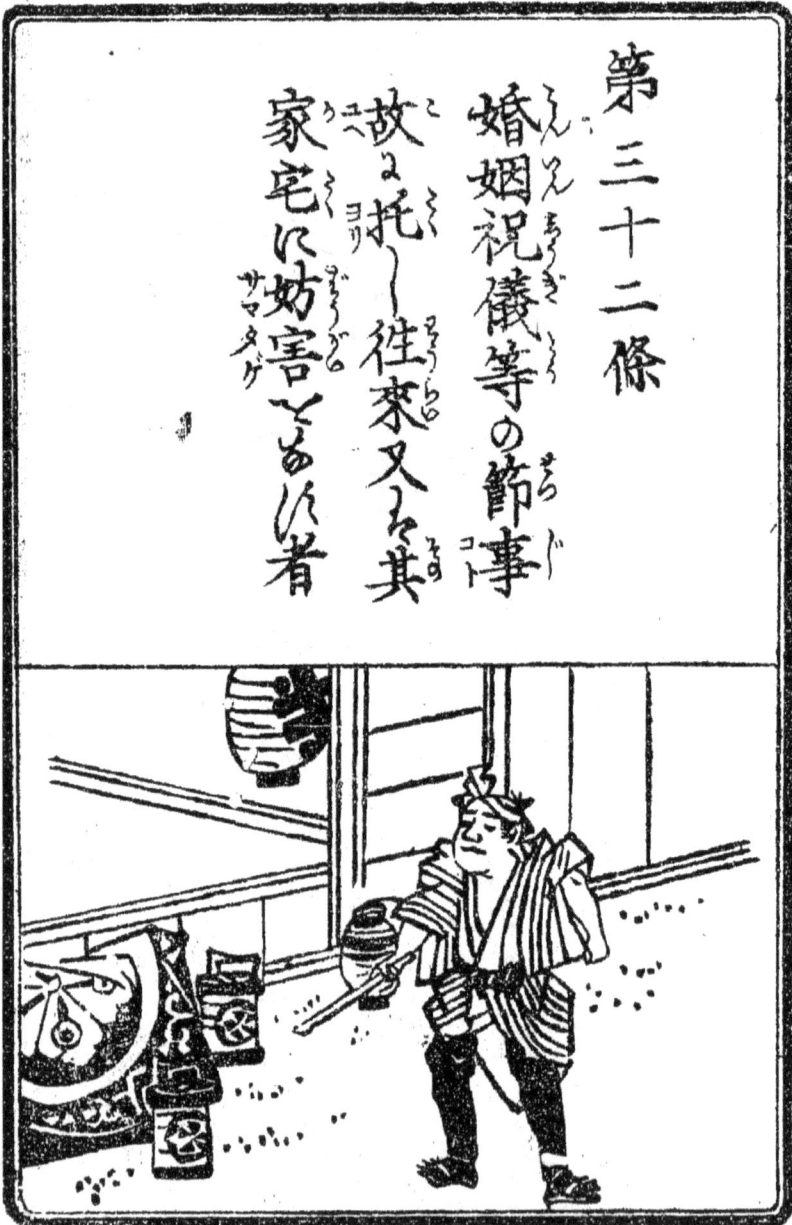

#32

Any person who blocks access to a road or house due to a wedding or other celebration is in violation.

第三十三條

馬夫或ハ日雇稼の者
等仲間ヲ結び他人
の稼とあたる故障
する者

#33

Packhorse drivers and day laborers who form a union, thereby preventing others from making a livelihood, are in violation.

第三十四條

神佛祭事に託し人を妨害なすに者

#34
Preventing people's freedom of movement due to activities related
to a Shinto or Buddhist festival means you are in violation.

第三十五條

往來のて死牛馬の皮を剥肉を屠る者

#35

Skinning a cow or horse you find dead on the side of the road and taking its meat is a violation.

第三十六條

他人の墓碑を毀損する者

#36

If you vandalize the grave or gravestone of another person you are in violation.

第三十七條

官有山林等ヲ禁制ノ榜示あるヲ犯せシ者

#37

Ignoring no trespassing signs on government managed mountains or forests is a violation.

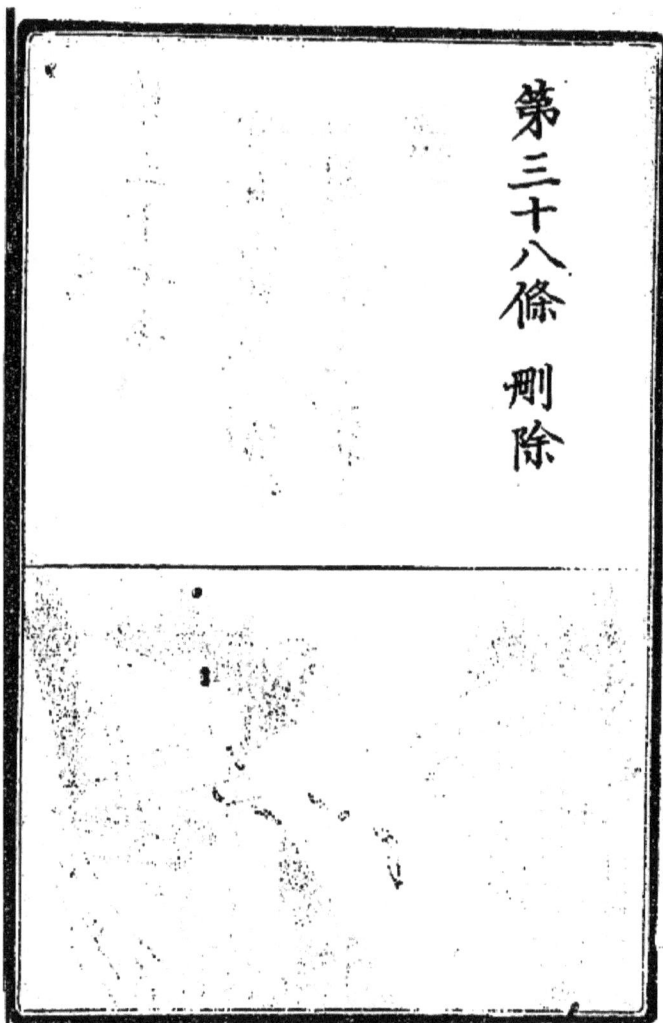

第三十八條 刪除

#38
This regulation has been eliminated.[6]

---

[6] This regulation originally read as follows:
#38
Anyone entering the fenced off area around a railway for the purpose of mischief is in violation.
It is not clear why this was eliminated.

第三十九條

御用と書たる小旗
提灯等と免許なく
猥りか用ある者

#39
Any person carrying a Kobata (Small Flag) or Chochin (Lantern)
with Goyo 御用 (Official Business) printed on it for a corrupt reason
is in violation.

#40

Untying a person's boat and taking it out on the water for your own entertainment without permission is a violation.

第四十一條

官有或ハ他人の山林
田畑に入植物を損害
そうる者

#41

Any person damaging or destroying plants on private property or in government managed mountains, forests, rice fields or vegetable fields is in violation.

#42

Anyone destroying or consuming the items in a Shrine or Temple is in violation.

第四十三條
狹隘（せまき）の小路（こうぢ）と馬車（むしゃ）にて馳走（ハシル）その者

The Following Offences are Classified as:
Mistakenly Violating the Rules

#43

Anyone driving a horse drawn carriage through a narrow street at high speed is in violation.

第四十四條

夜中無提灯にて諸車
と轅又ハ乗馬する者

#44
Anyone operating any kind of wheeled vehicle or riding horseback
at night without a Chochin, Lantern, is in violation.

#45
If you drive a horse drawn carriage at high speed without consideration, thereby endangering other passersby you are in violation.

第四十六條　馬車及び人力車荷
車等を往來に置行
人の妨げをなし及び牛
馬を街衢を横き行
人の妨げをなし者

#46

Anyone parking a horse drawn carriage, rickshaw or cart in a way that blocks the free movement of pedestrians is in violation. This also applies to people who tie up horses or cows in a way that prevents pedestrians from crossing the street.

第四十七條

禽獣の死るもの或ハ
汚穢の者を往來等ニ
投棄する者

#47
Anyone who disposes of a dead bird or animal in the street is in violation. This also applies to dumping any unclean thing in the street.

第四十八條

婦人みて謂違あく

断髪をる者

#48

A woman who cuts her hair without good reason is in violation.

Translator's Note: There were several laws passed against "unusual appearance." This included women cutting their hair short (like a man) as well as crossdressing. The illustrations below are from *Rules for Living in Kyoto* 京都府違式詿違条例 図解 published in Meiji 9 (1876.)

Rules for Living in Kyoto
#58
A woman who cuts her hair without reason is in violation.

#52: A man dressing as a woman or a woman dressing as a man is a violation. This applies to any strange manner of dress or decorating intended to expose people to a grotesque scene. However this of course does not apply to actors who perform Kabuki and dress as women and so forth.

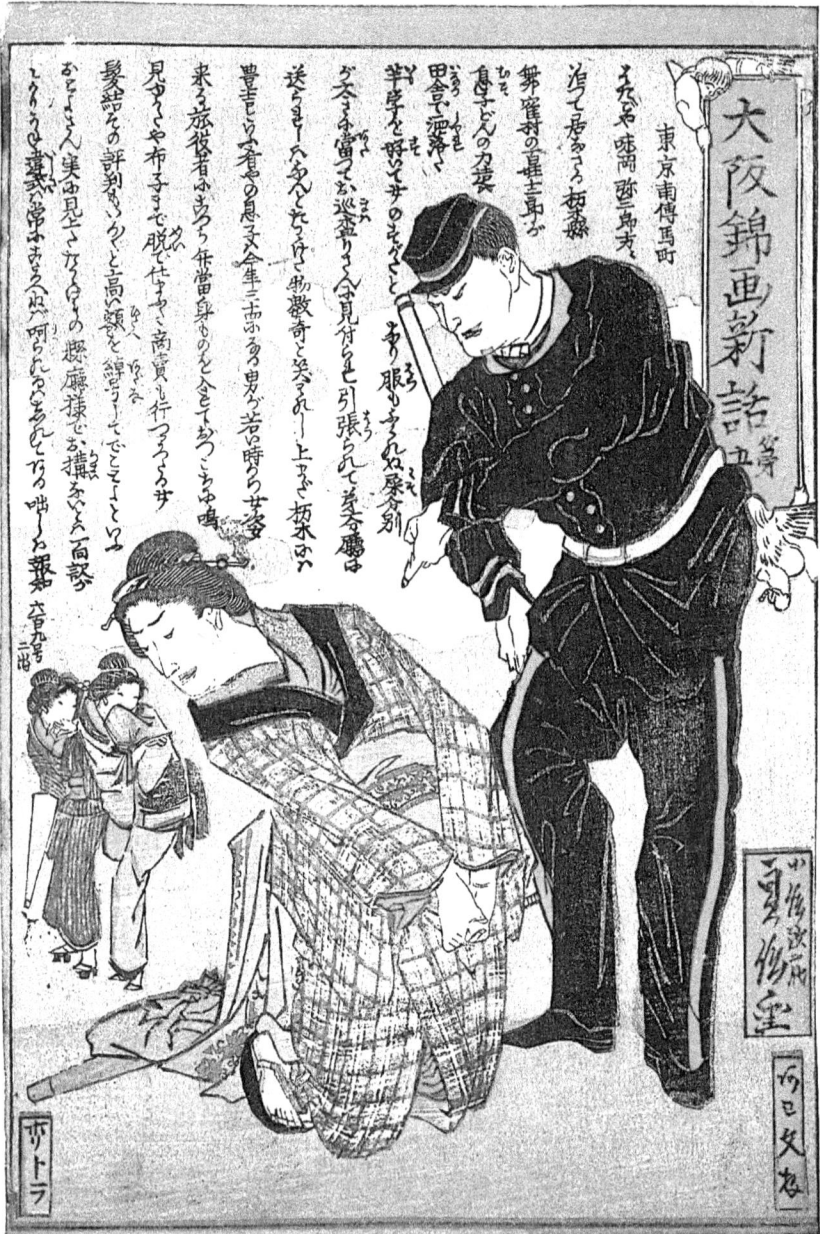

Osaka Illustrated Newspaper volume 5 大阪錦絵新話 5
(Publication date unknown, 1873~75)
A Junsa police officer is scolding a man dressed as a woman.

Tokyo Daily Newspaper 東京日々新聞
(Publication date unknown, 1873~75)
"An Officer questioning a Geisha dressed as a man. He takes her to
the station and fines her."
According to statistics published in Meiji 9, there were 8 violations
of this law. Either men dressing as women or women dressing as
men.

第四十九條

荷車及び人力車行
逢節行人の迷惑と
ろける者

#48

Two wagons or rickshaws crossing in opposite directions or stopping facing each other is a violation since it blocks the free movement of pedestrians.

第五十條

下掃除の者蓋おき
糞桶を以て搬運する
者

#48

Transporting night soil without covers on the buckets is a violation.

#51

If the proprietor of an inn does not record the names of guests or does not present his record book for inspection he is in violation.

第五十二條

往來筋の号札又ハ人家の番号名札看板等戯れに破毀する者

#52

Vandalizing or destroying the door numbers, nameplates, or signs on houses along a road is a violation.

喧嘩口論及び人の自由と妨げ且驚愕をぐき喧闘てお一出せる者

第五十三條

#53

Brawling and arguing as well as causing a scene is a violation. It impedes the free movement of people and causes a disturbance.

#54

Extinguishing or vandalizing a fixed lantern beside a road is a violation.[7]

---

[7] This seems to be the same as #19 however this illustration shows an adult, therefore the punishment is more severe.

#55
Carelessly throwing refuse, broken crockery or anything unclean at a person is a violation.

第五十六條

田園種藝の道あき場を通行し又ハ牛馬を牽入る者

#56

If there is no road, then walking through a rice field, garden or other cultivated area is a violation. This also includes leading a horse or cow through such an area.

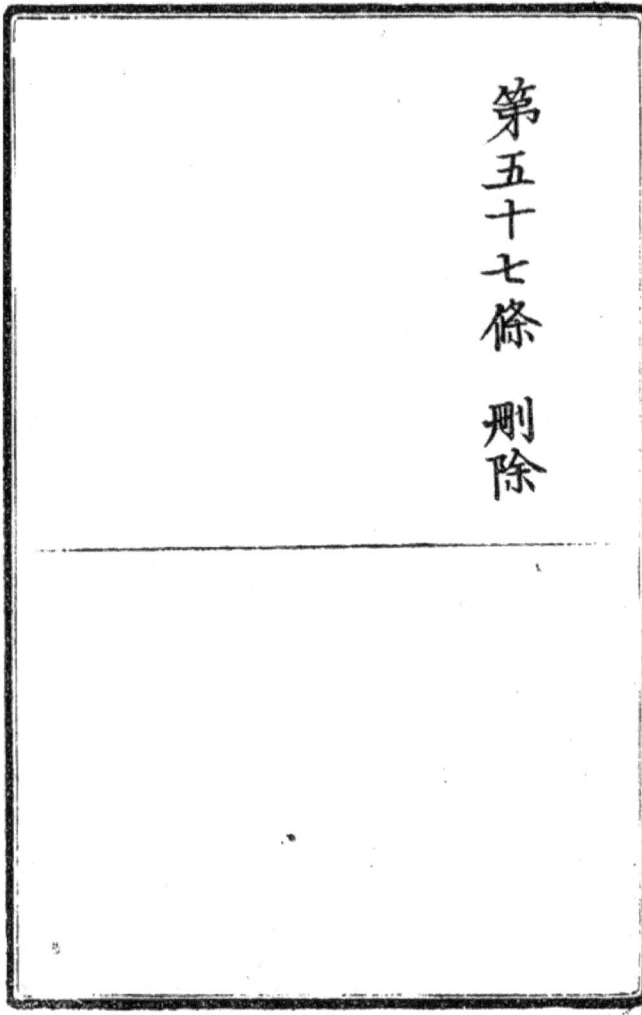

第五十七條　刪除

#57
This regulation has been erased.[8]

---

[8] This regulation originally read as follows:
#57
Anyone entangling the lines of an electric line is in violation.

Like regulation #38, it is not clear why this was eliminated.

第五十八條

荷車及び人力車等
と並び輓て通行と妨
一者

#58
Pulling two carts or rickshaws alongside each other is a violation because it blocks the free travel of others.

#59

Anyone who loses control of a horse or cow that enters a person's home is in violation.

第六十條

犬を闘いしめ及び
戯れに人を嗾る
者

#60

Any person encouraging dogs to fight is in violation. This includes
those who cause a dog to bite a person.

第六十一條

巨大の紙鳶を揚妨害致す者

#61
Any person who flies a giant paper kite which blocks people's free access to an area is in violation.

Illustration of people flying kites from *48 Famous Sights Around Tokyo* 東京名所四十八景 by Tatsuya Kichizo 蔦屋 吉蔵 1871

第六十二條

醉𛀙乘〜又ハ戲𛂞に
車馬住來の妨碍致
亦次者

#61
Any person who drunkenly blocks the passage of carts or rickshaws
is in violation. This includes blocking passage as a prank.

一 發狂人の看守を怠り路上ふ徘徊せしめたる者・

Translator's Note:
Regulations regarding drunkards were later expanded to include mentally ill persons.
This is from *Rules for Living in Osaka.* published in 1882:
Anyone responsible for a person who has gone insane and allows them to wander around the road is in violation.

#63
Any person who interferes with the operation of a place that dries
Zako, Assorted Small Fish, is in violation.

#64
Any person who interferes with the operation of a place that dries Nori, Seaweed, is in violation.

#65

Any person who interferes with another person's fishing nets or fish traps is in violation.

第六十六條

養田水其外用水ノ妨害ヲナス者

#66

Any person who interferes with water storage fields or other irrigation equipment is in violation.

第六十七條

水除杭ヲ妨害セ届又ハ引ヌキ等ヲ技取者

#67

Any person who interferes with stakes set to hold water back is in violation. This includes removing the stakes.

第六十八條
他人の竹木に妨害被
あし又ハ枝葉を拾ひ
取者
る

#68

Any person who interferes with another person's bamboo or trees is in violation. This also includes collecting branches or leaves.

他人の猟場を妨害て
第六十九條
その者

#69
Any person who interferes with another person's hunting grounds is
in violation.

#70

Any person who damages or destroys a person's garden fence or bamboo plant supports is in violation.

#71

A boat or ferry operator who charges an inappropriate amount is in violation. This also applies to operators who force passengers to wait an excessive amount of time, therefore interfering with their business.

第七十二條

往還の並木及び齣木
と徒らふ害とる者

#72

Any person damaging rows of trees or saplings along the side of the
road is in violation.

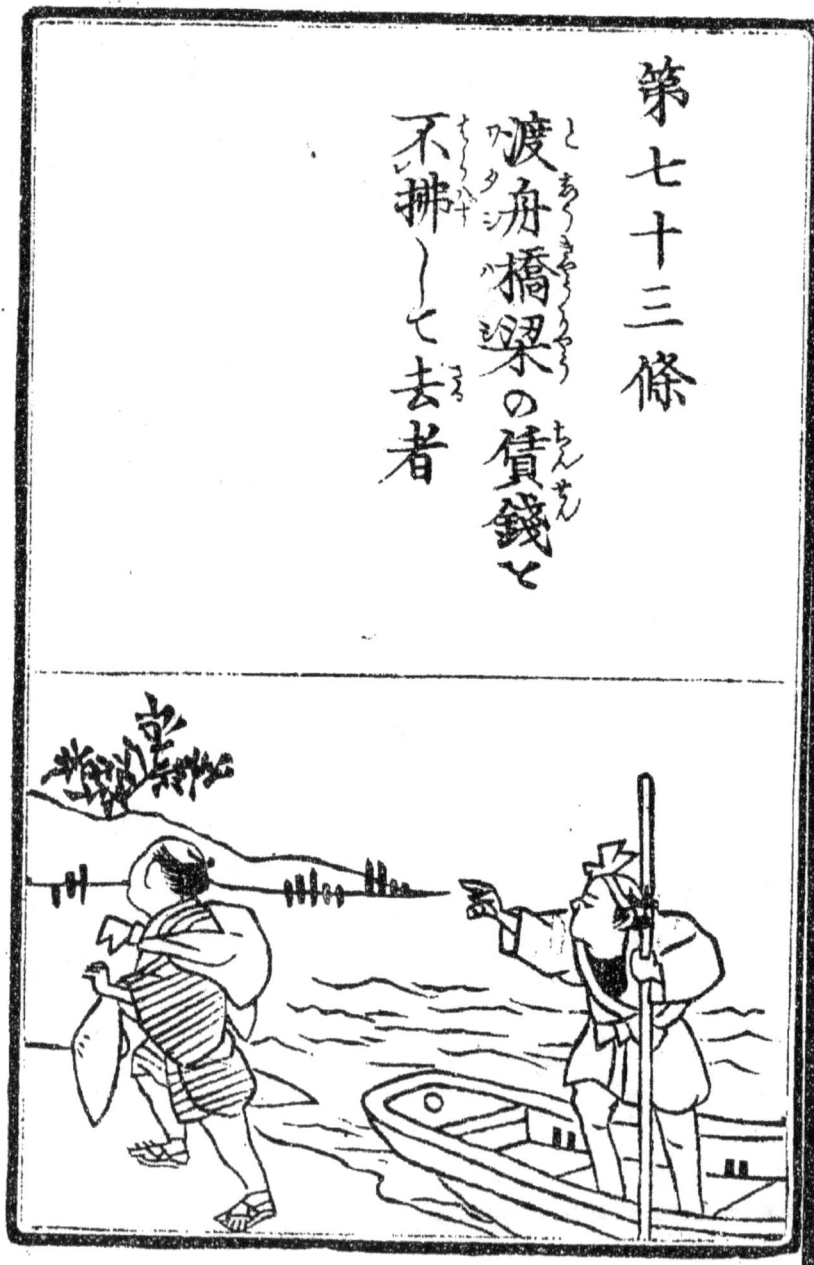

第七十三條

渡舟橋梁の賃銭を
不拂して去者

#73
Any person failing to pay a ferryman or bridge-man is in violation.

第七十四條

誤りて牛馬を放ち他人の田圃及び物品を損害する者

#74

Accidentally losing control of a horse or cow that charges into someone's rice field and proceeds to fuck everything up and break a bunch of shit is in violation.

#75
Joining an argument between two people you don't know for the purpose of inflaming tensions is a violation.

第七十六條
行人ニ合力等と軒
懸る者

#76

It is illegal to beg for money or assistance from travelers.

第七十七條

牧場外猥りに牛馬と

放し飼にする者

#77
Carelessly allowing the horses or cows you are raising to graze in a place other than a farm is a violation.

#78

Encouraging your dog to bite another person's pets or livestock is a violation.

第七十九條
他人の墳墓等の供品
類を猥りに毀損する
者

#79
Damaging or destroying someone's gravestone or the objects placed on the grave is a violation.

Later additions to the law included numerous entries on the handling of the deceased. These four entries are from *Mid-Level Police Violations* 刑法中違警罪図解. Kyoto 1882.

#7 Anyone dissecting a body without official permission is in violation.

#8 Failing to report a body on your property to the authorities or transporting a body to another area is a violation.

#9 Burying a person who died under unusual circumstances without notifying an official is a violation.

#10 Burying a body without reporting the death is a violation.

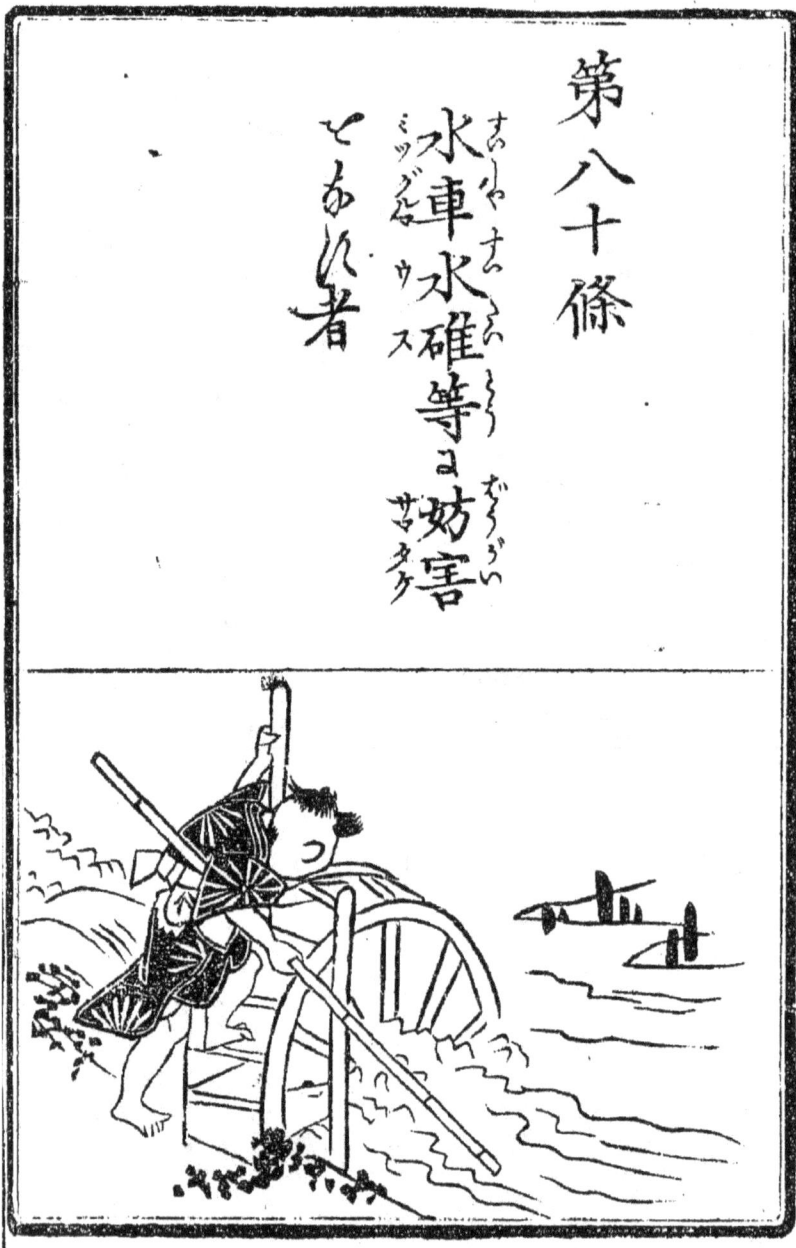

#80
Damaging or destroying a water wheel or water mill is a violation.

第八十一條

行人ヲ強ヒテ車馬駕籠
等ニ勧メ過言ヲ以申
懸ル者

#80

Using forceful tactics and strong words on pedestrians to get them
to ride in a rickshaw, palanquin or on a horse is a violation.

第八十二條

他人の曝網に妨害と

か沢者

#82
Damaging or destroying another person's fishing nets is a violation.

第八十三條
他人の海苔柵内へ断なく舩に掉さし入る者

#83
Using a boat to pole into another person's fenced off a seaweed farm is a violation.

#84
Making a fire in the mountains, forests or fields for no particular
purpose is a violation.

第八十五條

總ての標柱に牛馬と
繋ぎ或は破毀をる
者

#85

Tying your animal to a route marker or direction post is a violation.
This includes if you damage one of the posts.

#86

Tying a raft or boat to the supporting columns of a bridge is a violation.

第八十七條

神祠佛堂又ハ他人の垣壁に樂書をかき者

#87

Writing graffiti on a Shinto shrine, Buddhist temple or the wall around another person's house is a violation.

The two illustrations below are Heian Era (8th ~12th century) graffiti found in 平安時代に Taima Temple 当麻寺	

This is Nara Era (8th century) graffiti found in Horyuji Temple 法隆寺	Edo Era graffiti found in Matsuyama Castle

#88
Throwing pieces of roof tile, rocks, sticks or pieces of bamboo into a rice field or other cultivated land is a violation.

#89
Damaging or destroying the flowers or trees in a walk-through garden or along the side of the road is a violation.

第九十條

往來並木の枝に古草鞋と投、つける者

#90

Throwing your old Waraji, Woven Straw Sandals, into the branches of a tree along the side of a road is a violation.

官許明治七年七月

遠藤先生編輯

田中氏藏版

東京日本橋四日市

和泉屋半兵衛發兌

Approved by the Government
July of Meiji 7
Edited by Endo Sensei
Published in Tokyo

Translator's Note:

According to the *Tokyo Prefectural Statistics* 東京府統計表, in Meiji 9 (1876) there were 10,960 people fines for either *Disregarding the Rules* or *Mistakenly Violating the Rules*. The top 5 for each category are as follows:

Disregarding the Rules

1. Being nude or partially nude and thereby presenting an unseemly appearance.
   2,091 cases.
2. Pulling a rickshaw or riding a horse down a road closed to such.
   206 cases.
3. Pulling a rickshaw or riding a horse at high speed and knocking a person down.
   48 cases.
4. A person who embroiders (tattoos) their body.
   44 cases.
5. A person who harvests bamboo or timber or fishes or hunts in a forbidden area.
   40 cases.

Mistakenly Violating the Rules

1. Urinating in a place where urinating is not allowed.
   4495 cases.
2. Fighting or arguing or generally causing a disturbance.
   2727 cases.
3. Operating a carriage, rickshaw or cart at night without a lantern.
   506 cases.
4. Rickshaw drivers forcing people to use their service.
   109 cases.
5. Allowing a child to urinate in front of a business.
   101 cases.

Publishers in other prefectures sometimes copied the art without citing the source to make their own editions. Below the edition for Tochigi Prefecture copied the illustrations from the Tokyo edition.

違式詿違御條目図解全 Rules for Living in Tokyo 1874	栃木県違式詿違条例図解 Rules for Living in Tochigi 1878

118

www.ingramcontent.com/pod-product-compliance
Lightning Source LLC
Chambersburg PA
CBHW050350280326
41933CB00010BA/1406